WEIRD-BUT-TRUE FACTS ABOUT U.S. PRESIDENTS

BY ARNOLD RINGSTAD • ILLUSTRATED BY MERNIE GALLAGHER-COLE

The Child's World

Published by The Child's World®
1980 Lookout Drive • Mankato, MN 56003-1705
800-599-READ • www.childsworld.com

Acknowledgments
The Child's World®: Mary Berendes, Publishing Director
Red Line Editorial: Editorial direction
The Design Lab: Design
Amnet: Production

ISBN 9781614734222
LCCN 2012946529

Printed in the United States of America
Mankato, MN
November, 2012
PA02143

About the Author

Arnold Ringstad lives in Minneapolis, Minnesota. He wishes he could bowl with Richard Nixon, play marbles with John Adams, and call Rutherford B. Hayes on the telephone.

About the Illustrator

A former greeting card artist, Mernie Gallagher-Cole is a freelance illustrator with over 28 years experience illustrating for children. Her charming illustrations can be found on greeting cards, party goods, games, puzzles, children's books, and now e-books and educational game apps! She lives in Philadelphia with her husband and two children.

TABLE OF CONTENTS

INTRODUCTION

The president of the United States has been called the most powerful person on the planet. Forty-three men held the office from George Washington to Barack Obama. They have been young and old, tall and short, remembered and forgotten. And they all have been unique in one way or another. Get ready to learn odd facts about the presidents—and remember, they are all true!

PRESIDENTIAL FIRSTS

Rutherford B. Hayes was the first president to have a telephone.

It was installed in 1877. His telephone number was 1.

Jimmy Carter was the first president born in a hospital.

He was born in Plains, Georgia, in 1924. Presidents before him were born at home, like most people at that time.

John Quincy Adams was the first president to have his picture taken.

He posed for an early type of photograph in 1843.

Theodore Roosevelt was the first president both to ride publicly in an automobile and to ride in an airplane.

He rode in an electric car during a Connecticut parade in 1902. He took a four-minute flight in 1910 after leaving the presidency. The first president to fly while in office was Franklin Delano Roosevelt. Theodore Roosevelt was also the first president to leave the country while in office. He visited Panama.

Abraham Lincoln, elected in 1860, was the first president to have facial hair.

As of 2012, William Howard Taft, elected in 1908, was the last to wear a beard or mustache.

Benjamin Harrison was the first president to attend a baseball game.

He watched the Cincinnati Reds defeat the Washington Senators in the summer of 1892.

1860

1908

Rutherford B. Hayes was the first president to visit the West Coast.

He visited San Francisco in 1880 as part of a U.S. tour.

Barack Obama was the first president to regularly use e-mail in office.

PRESIDENTIAL PASTIMES

Zachary Taylor let his horse graze on the White House lawn.

The horse's name was Old Whitey.

Calvin Coolidge owned a **pygmy** hippo.

His other pets included six dogs, a cat, two raccoons, a donkey, a goose, a bobcat, two lion cubs, and an antelope.

Ronald Reagan bought 3.5 tons (3.5 t) of jelly beans to pass out at his inauguration parties.

Blue jellybeans were specially made so that there could be red, white, and blue jellybeans at the event.

Woodrow Wilson brought in sheep to keep the grass cropped short.

He used them to save money on landscaping during World War I (1914–1918).

Woodrow Wilson painted his golf balls black during the winter.

He did it so that he could keep playing when there was snow on the ground.

Harry S. Truman installed a bowling lane at the White House.

Richard Nixon later updated it and often enjoyed bowling with his wife, Pat.

George H. W. Bush celebrated his 85th birthday by skydiving.

He had jumped out of a plane years earlier, but not for fun. He parachuted into the sea when his bomber was shot down during World War II (1939–1945).

George Washington, John Adams, and Thomas Jefferson all enjoyed playing and collecting marbles.

Lyndon B. Johnson installed a soft drink button on his desk.

When he wanted his favorite soft drink, he pressed the button, and his assistant would bring him a drink.

PRESIDENTIAL TALENTS

Andrew Johnson only wore suits he made himself.

He is the only president who was once a tailor. Harry S. Truman owned a haberdashery, or a store that sells hats.

Made for Andrew Johnson by Andrew Johnson

James Garfield knew both the Latin and ancient Greek languages.

He could write in Latin with one hand and in Greek with the other hand at the same time.

Dwight Eisenhower earned a pilot's license in 1939.

Eisenhower was a military general before he was president. He was the commander of U.S. and Allied troops at the end of World War II (1939–1945). He was the first president to have a pilot's license.

Ronald Reagan was a famous actor before he got into politics.

He appeared in Western films in the 1940s and 1950s.

Abraham Lincoln held a license to sell liquor.

He was the co-owner of Berry and Lincoln, a **saloon** in Illinois.

Jimmy Carter was a peanut farmer in Georgia before becoming president.

Theodore Roosevelt gave a campaign speech immediately after being shot in 1912.

The bullet was slowed by a 50-page speech and a metal eyeglasses case in Roosevelt's pocket, but it still entered his body. The bullet remained in his body until his death in 1919.

Thomas Jefferson was a politician, a **philosopher**, a scientist, an inventor, a farmer, and a lawyer.

He also played three instruments, translated books, and founded the University of Virginia.

Abraham Lincoln was the only president to have a **patent** on an invention.

He invented a device to help move boats over sand bars in shallow water in 1849.

THE WHITE HOUSE

It takes **570** gallons of paint to paint the outside of the **White House**.

The White House receives 65,000 letters, 100,000 e-mails, 1,000 faxes, and 3,000 phone calls every day.

The White House has 132 rooms.

The total floor space adds up to about 55,000 square feet (5,100 sq m), more than 20 times bigger than the average house.

The president gets a dinner bill.

White House residents pay for their own food and miscellaneous items including toothpaste and dry cleaning. However, the government covers the cost of official banquets and functions.

Not all White House parties have been elegant and refined.

After Andrew Jackson's inauguration, huge crowds rushed into the White House to celebrate. The partiers broke dishes and glassware, and the new president escaped from the crowd through a window.

The White House kitchen can prepare dinner for up to 140 guests.

It also can serve snacks to 1,000 people.

The White House includes a swimming pool, a basketball court, and a movie theater.

Bill Clinton put in a jogging track and renovated Dwight Eisenhower's practice golf putting green in 1996. However, the track was paved over in 2008 as the grounds continue frequently changing.

FURTHER FASCINATING FACTS

James Madison was the shortest president. Abraham Lincoln was the tallest.

Madison stood at 5 feet, 4 inches (1.6 m), and Lincoln was 6 feet, 4 inches (1.9 m).

Six presidents were named "James."

They were Madison, Monroe, Polk, Buchanan, Garfield, and Carter.

The "S" in Harry S. Truman doesn't stand for anything.

The initial honors both of his grandfathers, Anderson Shipp Truman and Solomon Young.

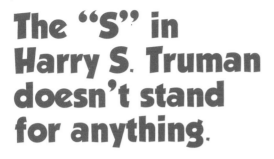

Richard Nixon made a phone call to the moon.

He spoke to Neil Armstrong and Buzz Aldrin after they landed on the moon in 1969. Nixon said it was "the most historic telephone call ever made from the White House."

George Washington's inaugural address was only 135 words.

It was the shortest in history. The longest was William Henry Harrison's. It was 8,445 words, and it took 105 minutes to read.

Warren G. Harding played poker often.

He once gambled away a set of White House dishes.

Thomas Jefferson introduced french fries to the United States.

He served them at a dinner in 1802.

George W. Bush once worked as a manager of the Texas Rangers baseball team.

In the summer of 1790, George Washington spent $200 on ice cream.

He served it to guests in tiny cups. At that time, all ice cream was fruit flavored. Vanilla and chocolate ice cream hadn't been invented yet.

Gerald Ford could have been a professional football player.

He played the sport at the University of Michigan, and he was offered contracts from the Detroit Lions and the Green Bay Packers. He decided to study law at Yale University instead.

As a child, Harry S. Truman often woke up at five o'clock in the morning to practice the piano.

William Henry Harrison was president for only 30 days.

He developed **pneumonia** after giving his inaugural address and died four weeks later.

Thomas Jefferson had two grizzly bears as pets.

The famous explorer Zebulon Pike gave them to the president as a present. However, Jefferson quickly decided he could not keep them, and he sent them to live in a natural history museum in Pennsylvania.

The noses of the presidents carved into Mount Rushmore are each 20 feet (6 m) long.

Their eyes are 11 feet (3 m) across. If the presidents' entire bodies were depicted on the monument, they would stand 465 feet (142 m) tall.

James Garfield was the first left-handed president.

He was the twentieth president. However, four of the last five presidents (through Barack Obama) have been left-handed.

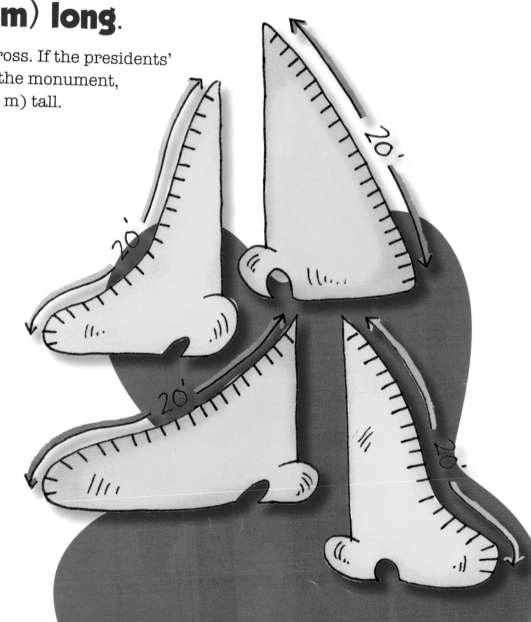

Ulysses S. Grant received a speeding ticket while president.

He was driving his horse and buggy too quickly down the street in Washington, DC.

George Herbert Walker Bush was the only president with four names.

Ye Olde Speeding Ticket

GLOSSARY

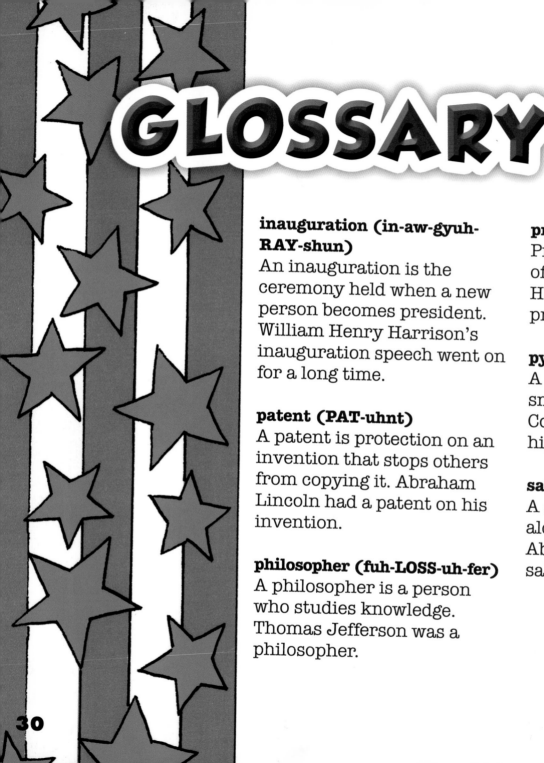

inauguration (in-aw-gyuh-RAY-shun)
An inauguration is the ceremony held when a new person becomes president. William Henry Harrison's inauguration speech went on for a long time.

patent (PAT-uhnt)
A patent is protection on an invention that stops others from copying it. Abraham Lincoln had a patent on his invention.

philosopher (fuh-LOSS-uh-fer)
A philosopher is a person who studies knowledge. Thomas Jefferson was a philosopher.

pneumonia (noo-MOH-nyuh)
Pneumonia is an illness of the lungs. William Henry Harrison died from pneumonia.

pygmy (PIG-mee)
A pygmy is an animal much smaller than usual. Calvin Coolidge owned a pygmy hippopotamus.

saloon (suh-LOON)
A saloon is a bar where alcoholic drinks are served. Abraham Lincoln owned a saloon in Illinois.

LEARN MORE

BOOKS
Lederer, Richard.
Presidential Trivia. Salt
Lake City, UT: Gibbs Smith,
2007.

McCullough, Noah.
*The Essential Book of
Presidential Trivia*.
New York: Random House
Trade Paperbacks, 2006.

WEB SITES
Visit our Web site for links
about weird U.S. president
facts: **childsworld.com/links**

*Note to Parents, Teachers, and
Librarians: We routinely verify our
Web links to make sure they are safe
and active sites. So encourage your
readers to check them out!*

INDEX